SKYSCRAPERS
BY CASS R. SANDAK

An Easy-Read Modern Wonders Book

FRANKLIN WATTS
New York / London / Toronto / Sydney
1984

Over: Workers stand on temporary flooring high above street level. Brave construction workers who build skyscrapers are sometimes called steeplejacks.

For Frank

R.L. 3.9 Spache Revised Formula

Cover photograph courtesy of Frank Sloan

Photographs courtesy of: Ewing Galloway: pp. 1, 11 (right), 19 (bottom), 21 (top), 26, 29 (bottom right); Frank Sloan: pp. 4, 9 (right), 10 (left), 13, 15, 17 (left), 18, 23 (right), 24 (top right and bottom), 29 (top); New York Convention & Visitors Bureau: pp. 6 (left), 7 (top right), 19 (top); the author: pp. 7 (top left and bottom left), 9 (left), 10 (right), 21 (left and right), 23 (left and right), 25 (left), 27 (left and right), 29 (bottom left); North Dakota Tourism Promotion: p. 7 (bottom right); The Bettmann Archive: pp. 8 (top), 17 (right); American Museum of Natural History: p. 8 (bottom left); Smithsonian Institute, Bureau of American Ethnology: p. 8 (bottom right); New York Public Library: p. 11 (left); Chicago Historical Society: p. 12 (left and right); Port Authority of New York and New Jersey: pp. 16, 24 (top left); Shostal Associates: p. 25 (right).

Diagrams by Jane Kendall

Library of Congress Cataloging in Publication Data

Sandak, Cass R.
   Skyscrapers.

  (An Easy-read modern wonders book)
  Includes index.
  Summary: Discusses the development of skyscrapers, how they are constructed, and new techniques for building them.
  1. Skyscrapers—Juvenile literature. [1. Skyscrapers] I. Title. II. Series.
NA6230.S26 1984   721'.042   84-2313
ISBN 0-531-04711-3

Copyright © 1984 by Cass R. Sandak
Printed in the United States of America
All rights reserved
6 5 4 3 2 1

Contents

Reach for the Sky	5
What Is a Skyscraper?	6
Tall Buildings Through the Ages	8
Making Skyscrapers Possible	10
The First Skyscrapers	12
Parts of a Skyscraper	14
Before Building Begins	18
Foundations	20
Superstructure	22
Heavy Equipment	24
New Construction Methods	25
Finishing Touches	26
Life Inside	28
Higher and Higher	29
Words About Skyscrapers	30
Index	32

Reach for the Sky

Skyscrapers are tall buildings that seem to stretch the mind and the imagination.

Even the beginning of a skyscraper is exciting. The high wooden fence that surrounds the construction site arouses curiosity. A "window" in the fence may give a glimpse of the skyscraper taking shape. Day by day passersby will be able to watch the building grow.

Once the skyscraper is finished, visitors to the building will have the thrill of riding high-speed elevators between floors. And on a clear day, people who look out from the top floors of the building may be able to see 40 or 50 miles (64 to 80 km) into the surrounding countryside. Objects in the street hundreds of feet below look like toys. And people look like tiny insects crawling about.

Skyscrapers turn our city streets into canyons of steel, glass, and stone. For a few people skyscraper walls that rise like cliffs hundreds of feet into the air present another type of challenge. Adventurers often try to scale the walls of a skyscraper as if they were the sides of a mountain.

No one can ignore a skyscraper.

A skyscraper under construction. The outer walls have been put on at the lower level, while the steel framework is still visible at the top of the building. The vertical shafts on the outside of the building hold elevators to transport workers and material to the top floors.

What Is a Skyscraper?

Skyscraper is a popular name for a tall building. In the 1840s the name was used to mean a number of different things. The highest sail of a ship, a tall person, a "tall" story, or any building higher than its neighbors all might be called skyscrapers.

The first true skyscrapers were ten or twelve stories high. Today's skyscrapers usually have at least fifty stories.

Modern skyscrapers are built to be practical and comfortable. They take avantage of small plots by stacking up floor upon floor of usable space for living and working. Land in the city is expensive and so it is cheaper to build up. Thousands of people can live or work in a tall

Two of New York City's famous skyscrapers. A skyscraper may take three years or more to build. *Left*: the Empire State Building was built in less than a year. *Right*: the World Trade center took more than six years to plan and build.

building that takes up only a small amount of land space.

Skyscraper office buildings, apartments, and hotels have long been a feature of American cities. More and more schools, universities, and hospitals are also in tall buildings. And there are churches located in skyscrapers.

The skyscraper is an American invention. And it is a true newcomer in the world of building. The world's first skyscraper was put up in 1884. A hundred years may sound like ages ago, but it really isn't such a long time in the history of building.

Two views of New York City, one by day and one by night. Well-known skyscrapers are visible from many miles away. Their outlines make up the city's skyline.

Two different uses of tall buildings. *Left*: the Cathedral of Learning is the University of Pittsburgh's skyscraper "classroom." *Right*: the "Skyscraper of the Prairies," North Dakota's capitol building in Bismarck.

One of the oldest stories in the Bible tells of mankind's attempt to build a tower reaching to heaven, the famous Tower of Babel.

Tall Buildings Through the Ages

In the New World the stepped pyramids of ancient Mexico (*left*) were early multistory structures. In the American Southwest, the Pueblo Indians built tiered homes (*right*).

Skyscrapers were not the first tall buildings. Even 5,000 years ago, builders tried to make their cities impressive with high walls and lofty towers.

Early palaces were built tall to take advantage of air and light above the crowded streets. Especially in the Middle East, the highest rooms were most prized because they let breezes pass through and were cooler in the warm climate.

Two thousand years ago Rome and its suburbs became so crowded that apartment buildings six or seven stories high were built. **Multistory** caves in Turkey and in southern France have been occupied since the time of Christ.

Because wood burns easily, it is not a good material for large buildings. Early buildings were almost always made of stone or brick. As buildings grew higher, they had to be supported by heavy stone walls. When buildings rose above six stories, they became so heavy that the walls at the base had to be very thick. That left little floor space for the lower stories.

Pagodas, the high temple buildings of China and Japan, give us a hint about the type of construction that was later used in skyscrapers. A **framework** of stone and wood enclosed by thin walls lets these structures rise to about ten stories.

Many cathedral spires, made entirely of stone, were more than 300 feet (90 m) high. *Left*: Lincoln Cathedral in England. *Right*: The Pittsburgh Plate Glass Center is a modern version of a cathedral tower in steel and glass.

Making Skyscrapers Possible

Three inventions made the development of the modern skyscraper possible: metal framework construction, steel, and elevators.

In the nineteenth century, iron frameworks were used for some buildings. **Cast iron** is a brittle material, but it can be easily molded. **Wrought iron** is a tougher and stronger material. The upright columns in the buildings were made of hollow cast-iron beams. Floor beams were made from wrought iron.

Two experimental structures helped make metal framework construction popular. The Crystal

Early uses of iron framework construction. *Left*: a cast-iron building in New York City. *Right*: an arched glass roof creates an inside open space inside a *galleria* in Naples, Italy.

Palace, in London, England, was a huge glass exhibition hall. It was built in 1851 around an iron framework. The Eiffel Tower was built in Paris, France, in 1889.

In the 1850s, the Englishman, Henry Bessemer, invented a better blast furnace that could make steel in large quantities. Steel is made by melting iron ore in a blast furnace. By increasing the flow of air into the hot mixture, the Bessemer furnace was able to burn away more impurities. This made higher grade steel. Because of its strength and flexibility, steel is highly prized. Steel beams make even better frameworks than iron.

The ancient Romans used small, hand-driven elevators made with ropes and pulleys. They carried food and supplies from one floor to another. But the first passenger elevator was only built in 1853. Elisha Otis's invention meant that people could reach the upper floors of a building without walking. In 1859, the Fifth Avenue Hotel in New York City became the first elevator building in the world. It was six stories high.

London's Crystal Palace (*left*) and Paris's Eiffel Tower (*right*) were not skyscrapers, but they showed that large structures could be built from an iron framework.

The First Skycrapers

Chicago

In the 1880s, Chicago, Illinois, was growing rapidly. A severe fire in 1871 had destroyed many buildings in the center of the city and new ones were needed.

In 1884, an architect named William LeBaron Jenney tried a tricky experiment. This resulted in the world's first true steel frame skyscraper. The building was started and the first six floors had already been built around an iron framework. Just at this time, steel beams made by the Bessemer process became available. Jenney finished the upper four stories of his Home Insurance Building with a framework of steel beams. This was the first use of steel in a multistory building. The idea caught on, and soon other architects were using steel frameworks in their buildings.

Left: Jenney's Home Insurance Building in Chicago. *Right*: Chicago's Monadnock Building under construction. This was the tallest skyscraper built without a metal framework. Massive stone walls bear the weight of the floors above.

New York

In the 1890s, architects in New York City built several metal frame skyscrapers that were between twenty and thirty stories high.

The Flatiron Building was one of the earliest and most important skyscrapers in New York City. It was designed for a triangular lot at 23rd Street and Broadway. Although the area of land was small, the building had to contain enough office space to make it profitable.

The 21-story Flatiron Building was finished in 1902. Soon New York City had a number of other skyscrapers. In 1909 the Metropolitan Life Insurance Building Tower was opened. It was over fifty stories high. And in 1913 the architect Cass Gilbert designed the 60-story Woolworth Building.

Today cities around the world boast skylines that are dominated by skyscrapers. Most new office and apartment buildings in modern cities are built by the steel framework method.

From left to right, three of New York City's most famous early skyscrapers: the triangular Flatiron Building; the Metropolitan Life Insurance Tower; and the Woolworth Building.

Parts of a Skyscraper

A skyscraper can be divided into two parts. The part below ground is called the **foundation**, or substructure. The part above the foundation is called the **superstructure**. The inside part of the superstructure is called the framework. The outside of the building is called the **exterior**, and the inside is called the **interior**.

Often the exterior walls of a skyscraper do not rise straight up to the top. The building rises a number of stories and there is a ledge. Above that ledge the building starts to rise again for another number of stories. These ledges look like steps and are called **setbacks**. Setbacks allow sunlight and air to reach the other buildings and streets that surround the skyscraper.

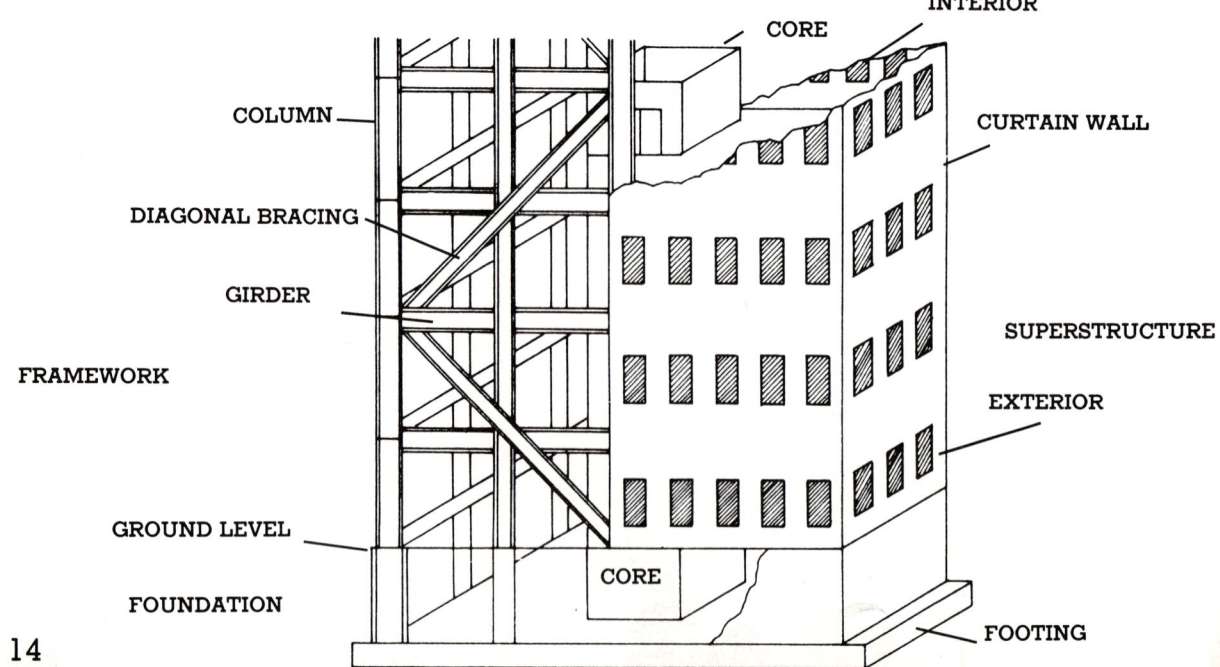

The older building in the center has prominent setbacks. Newer skyscrapers are usually built on vertical lines and are "set back" from the ground floor straight up.

A skyscraper is built around a steel skeleton framework. The upright posts of the framework are the **columns**. These are made from steel "H" beams. Smaller and lighter "I" beams form the horizontal crossbeams, or **girders**. The weight of the floors is carried by these steel beams joined together to form a cagelike framework.

The foundation spreads the weight of the building over a large area. The weight of a building is called the **load**. The building must be strong enough to support the **dead weight**, the weight of the building itself, and the **live load**. The live load is the weight of the building and all the people, furnishings, and equipment inside it. The weight is distributed evenly over the bottommost part of the foundation. These broad, thick concrete slabs are called the **footings**.

A building in Boston going up. *Left*: the uncompleted steel framework. *Right*: five months later, the framework is finished and the walls and window frames are being added.

An aerial view of the World Trade Center under construction. The tower at the bottom of the picture clearly shows the building's core (darkened portion) surrounded by the rest of the framework.

The pressure of wind can greatly increase the building's load. The **wind load** is the weight of the building when the wind blows against it. Most steel framework buildings have additional beams set diagonally in the framework. This **bracing** helps keep the framework rigid even in high winds.

Many recent skyscrapers are built around a **core.** The core of a skyscraper cannot be seen, but in many ways it is the most important part of the whole building. The core rises up from the foundation at the center of the building and continues throughout its height. It is like a backbone that gives the skyscraper its strength.

The core contains the strongest columns of the building. These are set within reinforced concrete walls that form a hollow tube with many openings. The core contains stairways and elevator shafts, pipes for water, sewage, gas, heating, air conditioning, and electric and telephone cables.

The outside walls of most skyscrapers do little more than keep the weather out. In most cases they are not **load-bearing** walls that hold up the floors above. Therefore they do not need to be thick. Large areas of the walls can be opened up for many windows. Walls like these are called **curtain walls**, since they are only thin coverings over the building's framework. The spaces between the beams and columns of the framework are often fitted with **infill panels** of glass, metal, brick, stone, or molded concrete.

Curtain walls of aluminum cover the outside of Pittsburgh's Alcoa Building (*left*). New York's Lever House (*right*) has outer walls mainly of green tinted glass.

Before Building Begins

The planning of a skyscraper begins with a study of the **site plan** and then the preparation of a complete building design. Will people live there? Will people work there? What other uses will the building have? All these questions must be answered.

The architects and designers must know about the building materials they will use. Problems with rust, moisture, air pollution, stress, and metal fatigue will have to be solved.

Architects will make hundreds of drawings that show every part of the building in detail. Modern skyscraper design is simple and most often uses straight lines.

Floor plans show the arrangement of rooms and open spaces for each floor. They show where doors and windows will be placed. The insides of most skyscrapers today are designed with an **open plan**. The center of each floor is taken up by the

Skyscraper design is often simple, but decoration sometimes adds interesting highlights. These colorful relief panels adorn New York's Graybar Building.

Modern architects plan not only the buildings but the land around them as well. Rockefeller Center in New York City was the first planned group of skyscrapers.

core. The rest of the floor can be divided in any way that is wished.

Site preparation begins with clearing the land where the skyscraper will be built. Workers may have to tear down buildings that already stand there.

Surveyors will ensure that property lines are correct and will locate the exact position for the new building. Finally steam shovels and bulldozers can go to work scooping out the vast hole needed to build the foundation for a modern skyscraper.

Left: A wrecking ball sends an old building crashing to the ground before a new one can be built. Old pipes and rubble will have to be cleared away from the building site.
Right: A building floor plan.

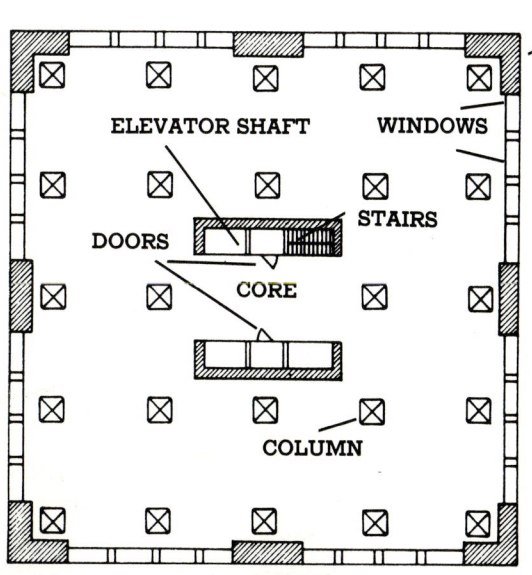

19

Foundations

A large building is a very heavy thing. The foundation bears the weight of the building. But before construction can begin, the makeup of the ground and rock below must be studied.

For the building to stand up straight, the foundation needs to be deep and solid. If the foundation is weak, the building may settle unevenly and the walls and foundation may crack.

A skyscraper's foundation is adapted to the conditions of the ground. In most places, several feet under the soil there is a solid layer of rock. Architects try to build their foundations on this **bedrock**.

In places where the bedrock is far below the surface of the soil, the foundations will have to be deep. Where the ground is soft, **piles**—long pillars of steel, concrete, or wood—may extend

Left, a pile foundation.

Right, a raft foundation.

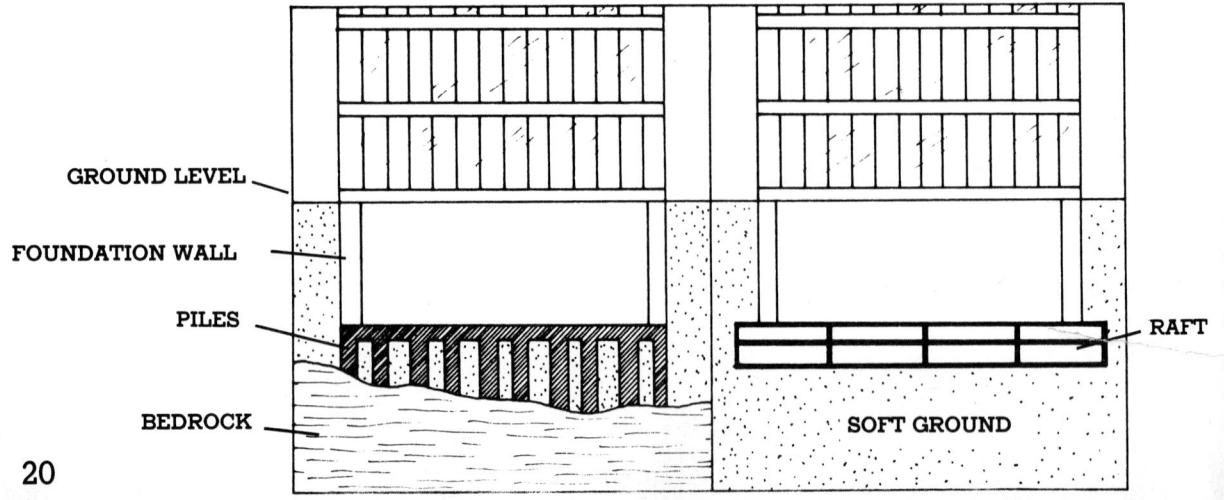

Workers pour concrete into the foundation of a large skyscraper. Today concrete is the main building material used for most skyscrapers.

many feet down into the ground. Piles help make a more solid base for the foundation.

Foundations need to be waterproof. Digging down in the earth is often like digging a well. If there is too much water, pumps may be needed to remove water. This is particularly true in the soggy ground near a river, lake, or ocean front. Sometimes the foundation walls are built almost like a dam to hold back water and soggy earth.

A skyscraper's foundation may create several underground stories. These basement levels can hold parking spaces, heating systems, storage rooms and other service areas.

Left: the foundation of a building under construction. *Right*: San Francisco's pyramid shaped TransAmerica Building was built to withstand earthquakes. The foundation would "float" on top of the subsoil in the event of an earthquake.

Superstructure

The columns at the bottom of a skyscraper are set on a heavy metal plate or stand on a footing of reinforced concrete. Or they may be bolted to a **grillage** that is set in the foundation.

A grillage is a framework made from layers of crisscrossed steel beams. Each column of the core stands on a grillage unit. Each grillage is set in a pit. Later the grillages and column bases will be embedded in concrete.

A framework of spaced steel beams carries the weight of most skyscrapers. The framework must be made of steel that is tough enough not to break under stress.

The vertical columns of the framework are usually "H" beams. They are made of thick steel and support the heaviest mass of the building. They are several inches wide and may be two or three stories long. As soon as two columns are in place, they are connected by crossbeams or girders that are usually "I" beams. More columns

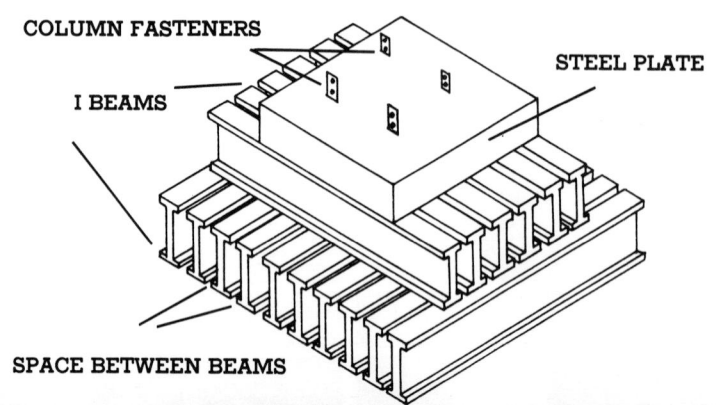

The grillage looks like a raft and is embedded in concrete. The grillage distributes the load evenly over the concrete footing.

Left: steel girders and columns are sprayed with fireproof material to make the building safe. *Right*: Chicago's 60-story Marina City. The core supports the floors that extend out around it like pine tree branches. This structural technique is called cantilevering. The apartments inside are wedge shaped.

and beams are added to make a boxlike framework.

A second series of upright columns is joined to the columns below it and more crossbeams are added. This process is repeated for each floor. The beams may be bolted together or **riveted**, with pins driven through them and flattened. Occasionally the framework is welded, using special torches that melt pieces of metal together.

Smaller "I" beams, called **filler beams**, are laid from one main girder to the next. The filler beams support the flooring. At first, temporary wooden floors are laid across from beam to beam. Then sheets of flat, heavy steel **decking** are put into place. This decking makes a form for pouring concrete floor slabs. Steel reinforcing rods make the floor stronger. The floor slabs and decking have openings to let electrical and telephone wires through.

I BEAM

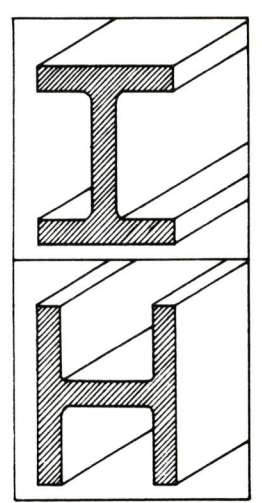

H BEAM

Left: kangaroo cranes were used on the World Trade Center. They have powerful jacks that let them jump up to the next floor as each new level is finished. *Right:* a giant crane alongside a skyscraper under construction.

Heavy Equipment

A **crane** is a movable lifting device. The framework, called the main boom, is used for support. The whip boom moves like a forearm and holds the lifting cables. A weight helps to balance the weight at the boom. A ball and hook dangle from the end of the lifting cable. The hook is used to hoist materials up to where they are needed on the framework.

Derricks are frameworks for lifting. They work like cranes but in a fixed position.

Concrete being poured into a bucket at street level. A crane will take the material up to where it is needed.

24

Left: the concrete core of a New York City hotel under construction. The floors will then be built around the core. *Right*: the Sears Tower in Chicago is the tallest building in the world. It was built by the tube framing method.

New Construction Methods

In many skyscrapers faster and cheaper methods are replacing the traditional steel framework construction. In **tube framing** the outer walls of the building form a strong, hollow tube or cylinder. Floors are supported on beam or truss sections between the core and outer walls. The World Trade Center was built this way.

In the **slip-form** process, wooden forms are filled with liquid concrete. This hardens to become the building's framework. As each new level is cast, the form is slipped off and used again. In the **lift-slab** method, each floor is constructed around the core and is then slid up and anchored in place.

A view from the observation deck of Boston's Prudential Center. Some skyscrapers have restaurants and shops at the top. Others have roof-level apartments called penthouses.

Finishing Touches

As soon as the framework for a floor is complete, finishing workers can install floors, walls, and windows. This will happen even while other parts of the framework are being riveted in place. Ironworkers may still be finishing the top of the building while the bottom floors are being fitted with plumbing and wiring.

Floor by floor the framework is finished. Putting the highest piece of steel in place is called **topping out**. Workers pause to celebrate. Then they go back to work.

The roof of a skyscraper does more than keep out rain and snow. Almost every skyscraper has a huge tank on top where water is stored for use in the sprinkler system or in an emergency. The motors for elevators are usually located on the roof. Electric pumps carry water to the roof and upper floors.

Today large sections of skyscrapers are **prefabricated**. This means that they are put together in a factory and then shipped to the building site. These sections include floors, ceilings, windows, and wall units. They are hoisted into position and bolted in place.

Windows are usually put in place from the outside. Sometimes workers have to dangle huge panes of glass from a derrick to position them.

Hundreds of workers with many different skills are needed to make the building comfortable. Carpenters, plumbers, plasterers, electricians, and phone workers are just some of them. Last of all, painters and decorators will ready the building for its occupants.

Left: the metal trusswork of a skyscraper ceiling. This framework will support soundproof tiles that cover pipes, heating ducts, wiring, and sprinkler systems. *Right*: a restaurant, walkway, and pond decorate the lower level of a Chicago hotel.

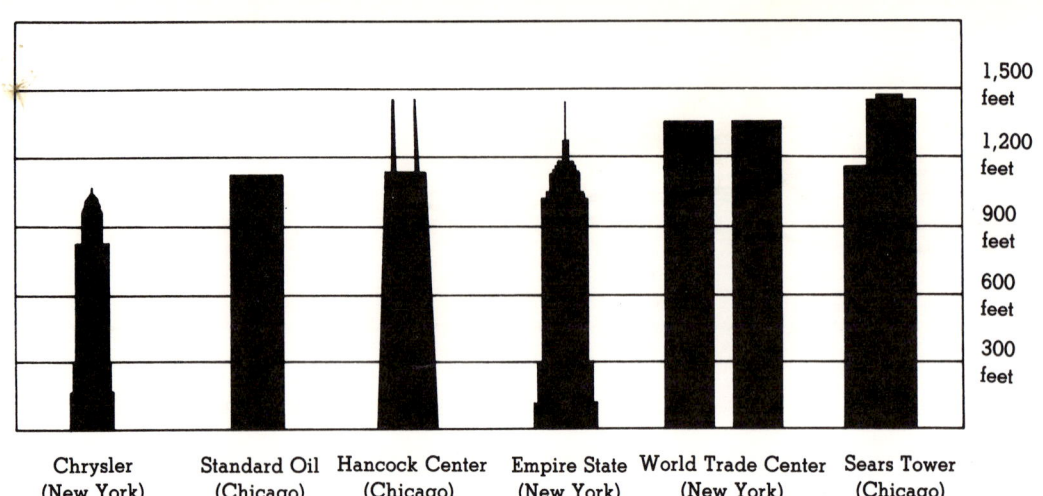

The world's tallest buildings

Chrysler (New York) | Standard Oil (Chicago) | Hancock Center (Chicago) | Empire State (New York) | World Trade Center (New York) | Sears Tower (Chicago)

Life Inside

Many complex systems are needed to keep a skyscraper usable and safe. A crew of workers is required to keep the building running smoothly. Maintenance people and cleaners work around the clock. Window washers risk their lives daily as they hang from leather belts hooked outside each window frame. Some new buildings have a window cleaning platform that hangs down from a track on the roof.

In some new buildings, computers help the structure to adjust to changes in wind pressure. Computers also control air quality and lighting automatically throughout the floors. Most new skyscrapers do not have windows that can be opened. Ventilating and air conditioning systems keep the building cool in summer and warm in winter. Alarm systems and closed-circuit TV screens help the building security staff.

The old and new, side by side. H.H. Richardson's County Court House in Pittsburgh sits next to the brand new Dravo Building.

Higher and Higher

The skylines of cities around the world are constantly changing. Taller and taller buildings are being planned and built every day. Architects are experimenting with bigger buildings, and they are trying new styles and building methods. Computers are used to design buildings and to run them once they are built. Planners try to arrange public gardens and recreational areas around skyscrapers. Modern skyscrapers help us to use our land and space better. And they will make tomorrow's cities even better places to work and live.

Changing skylines. Tehran, Iran (*left*) and Seattle, Washington (*right*) show the popularity of skyscrapers throughout today's world.

Words About Skyscrapers

Bedrock. A solid layer of rock under the surface of the earth.
Bracing. Diagonal beams to help make a framework rigid.
Cantilevering. A technique that lets floors extend out from a core, like a bracket bookshelf.
Cast iron. A type of iron that was used in early framework construction.
Column. An upright post of a steel framework.
Core. The center of a skyscraper. It is the backbone and strongest part of a building.
Crane. A movable lifting machine.
Curtain wall. An outside wall that is only a relatively thin covering over the framework. It does not support the framework.
Dead weight. The weight of a building itself.
Decking. Steel sheeting that supports concrete floor slabs.
Derrick. A framework for lifting heavy material into a skyscraper.
Elevation. A drawing that shows how the sides of a building will look.
Exterior. The outside of a building.
Filler beams. Small "I" beams used to connect girders.
Floor plans. Plans that show the floor layout of a building.
Footings. Concrete slabs that are the bottommost part of a foundation. They spread the building's weight over a large area.
Foundation. The part of a skyscraper below the ground.
Framework. A metal skeleton, around which a building is constructed.
Girder. A horizontal beam in a steel framework. Also called a crossbeam.

Grillage. A raftlike framework made from layers of crisscrossed steel beams.
Infill panel. Space between a beam and a column, fitted with glass, metal, or stone.
Interior. The inside of a building.
Lift-slab. A method of skyscraper construction. Each floor is built around the core and then slid up and fastened to the core.
Live load. The weight of a building and everything inside it.
Load-bearing walls. Walls that hold up the floors above.
Multistory. Having more than one story or floor.
Open plan. A plan that allows the floor of a skyscraper to be broken up in a variety of ways.
Penthouse. A luxurious apartment usually at the top of a tall building.
Piles. Pillars dug deep into the ground that help strengthen a building's foundation.
Setback. A ledge on a building. The floors above the ledge are set back from the floors below.
Site plan. A layout that shows where the skyscraper will be built.
Skyline. An outline of skyscraper shapes against the sky.
Slip-form. A method of construction. A form is filled with concrete and then slipped off and used on the next part.
Steeplejack. Construction workers who rivet skyscraper steel frameworks together.
Superstructure. The part of a skyscraper that is above the ground.
Topping out. Putting the highest piece of steel in place.
Trusswork. A light metal framework.
Wind load. The weight of a building when the wind blows against it.
Wrought iron. A metal used in early framework buildings.

Index

Bedrock, 20, 30
Bessemer, Henry, 10
Bracing, 16, 30

Cantilevering, 23, 30
Cast iron, 10, 30
Columns, 15, 30
Computer, use of, 28, 29
Construction methods, new, 25
Core, 16–17, 30
Crane, 24, 30
Curtain walls, 17, 30

Dead weight, 15, 30
Decking, 23, 30
Derricks, 24, 30

Elevators, 10, 30
Exterior, 14, 30

Filler beams, 23, 30
Finishing touches, 26–27
Floor plans, 18, 30
Footings, 15, 30
Foundations, 14, 20–21, 30
Framework, 9, 10, 30

Girders, 15, 30
Grillage, 22, 31

H beams, 22

I beams, 22
Infill panels, 17, 31
Interior, 14, 31

Jenney, William Le Baron, 12

Kangaroo cranes, 24

Life inside, 28
Lift-slab method, 25, 31
Live load, 15, 31
Load, 15
Load-bearing walls, 17, 31

Multistory caves, 9, 31

New York architecture, 13

Open plan, 18, 31
Otis, Elisha, 10

Pagodas, 9
Penthouses, 26, 31
Piles, 20–21, 31
Prefabricated sections, 27

Riveted, 23

Setbacks, 14, 31
Site plan, 18, 31
Site preparation, 19
Skylines, 7, 29, 31
Skyscrapers
   first, 7, 12–13
   parts of, 14–17
Slip-form process, 25, 31
Steel, 10, 12
Steeplejack, 31
Superstructure, 14, 22–23, 31
Surveyors, 19

Topping out, 26, 31
Trusswork, 31
Tube framing method, 25

Wind load, 16, 31
Wrought iron, 10, 31

J725   Sandak, Cass R.
SAN   Skyscrapers

	DATE		

FEB 8 5

NORTHPORT PUBLIC LIBRARY
NORTHPORT, NEW YORK

© THE BAKER & TAYLOR CO.